What's in the Bible About the Holy Spirit?

What's in the Bible,
and Why Should I Care?

What's in the Bible About the *the Holy Spirit*

Alex Joyner

ABINGDON PRESS
NASHVILLE

WHAT'S IN THE BIBLE ABOUT THE HOLY SPIRIT?
by Alex Joyner

 Abingdon Press

ISBN-13: 978-0-687-65284-6

Manufactured in the United States of America

08 09 10 11 12 13 14 15 16 17—10 9 8 7 6 5 4 3 2 1

CONTENTS

ABOUT THE WRITER

Alex Joyner is a United Methodist pastor serving on the Eastern Shore of Virginia, one of the last undeveloped coastal regions on the Eastern seaboard. Alex serves Franktown Church, a vibrant congregation representing the diversity of the region. In previous roles, he has worked in inner-city Dallas, Texas, as a youth director; as an associate pastor in a bilingual Latino congregation; as a pastor in England and Virginia; and as a campus minister at the University of Virginia. His experience with college students and young adults led him to write *Restless Hearts: Where Do I Go Now, God?* (Abingdon Press), a resource for discovering your vocation.

Alex has been a featured preacher on the former *Protestant Hour* radio broadcast (now *Day One*) and began his career as a radio news director. He is summer adjunct lecturer at Southern Methodist University, where he has taught Bible and theology courses since 1996. He has a great interest in missions and has led work teams domestically and in Mexico. He has also led a student group to two places of Christian pilgrimage—Taize, France, and Iona, Scotland.

Alex is an avid kayaker who is often found paddling in the marshes and bays near his home. He is married to Suzanne and has two children, Joel and Rachel.

About This Bible Study Series

Have you ever wondered what the Bible is all about? What's in it? Why is it so important for Christians? Is it relevant for people in the 21st century? Should I care about what's in the Bible? Why? What difference will it make in my life? The study series *What's in the Bible, and Why Should I Care?* offers opportunities for you to explore these questions and others by opening the Bible, reading it, prayerfully reflecting on what the Bible readings say, and making connections between the readings and your daily life. The series title points to the two essential features of meaningful Bible study: reading the Bible and applying it to your life. This unique and exciting Bible study series is designed to help you accomplish this two-fold purpose.

The books in *What's in the Bible, and Why Should I Care?* are designed to help you find relevance, hope, and meaning for your life even if you have little or no experience with the Bible. You will discover ways the Bible can help you with major questions you may have about the nature of God, how God relates to us, and how we can relate to God. Such questions continue to be relevant whether you are new to church life, a long-time member of church, or a seeker who is curious and wants to know more.

Whether you read a study book from this series on your own or with others in a Bible study group, you will experience benefits. You will gain confidence in reading the Bible as you learn how to use and study it. You will find meaning and hope in the people and teachings of the Bible. More importantly, you will discover more about who God is and how God relates to you personally through the Bible.

What's in the Bible?

Obviously, we answer the question "What's in the Bible?" by reading it. As Christians, we understand that the stories of our faith come to us through this holy book. We view the Bible as the central document for all we believe and profess about God. It contains stories about those who came before us in the Christian faith, but it is more than a book of stories about them. The Bible tells us about God. It tells how a particular group of people in a particular part of the world over an extended period of time, inspired by God, understood and wrote about who God is and how God acted among them. The Bible also tells what God expected from them. Its value and meaning reach to all people across all time—past, present, and future.

Why Should I Care?

Meaningful Bible study inspires people to live their lives according to God's will and way. As you read through the stories collected in the Bible, you will see again and again a just and merciful God who creates, loves, saves, and heals. You will see that God expects people, who are created in the image of God (Genesis 1), to live their lives as just and merciful people of God. You will discover that God empowers people to live according to God's way. You will learn that in spite of our sin, of our tendency to turn away from God and God's ways, God continues to love and save us. This theme emerges from and unifies all the books that have been brought together in the Holy Bible.

Christians believe that God's work of love and salvation finds confirmation and completion through the life, ministry, death, and resurrection of Jesus Christ. We accept God's free gift of love and salvation through Jesus Christ; and out of gratitude, we commit our lives to following him and living as he taught us to live. Empowered by God's Holy Spirit, we grow in faith, service, and love toward God and neighbor. I pray that this Bible study series will help you experience God's love and power in your daily life. I pray that it will help you grow in your faith and commitment to Jesus Christ.

Pamela Dilmore

They were tumultuous times. An empire many thought would never fall had retreated from the scene, leaving behind a world of uncertain alliances and economic turmoil. However, as the Romans left the British Isles in 405, a flicker of a new age remained. On the margins of Ireland, a group of Celtic monks was listening for God's voice and miraculous things were happening. The faith the Romans had brought was being reborn.

These Celtic Christians had incorporated the story of Jesus into their culture with unique images. One of them was the use of the wild goose as a symbol for the Holy Spirit, in contrast to the traditional symbol of the dove. With its awkward bearing and obnoxious honk, a goose seems a strange sign of the Spirit, God's continuing presence in the world. However, as Ron Ferguson noted in his study of the Iona Community, a contemporary Celtic Christian network, the wild goose is "a turbulent sign which is more appropriate to living the faith in our day than is the gentle dove. We live on a rollercoaster."[1]

One of the biblical phrases associated with the Holy Spirit, the third of the primary names by which Christians talk about God, is *the Comforter*. However, while Christians take comfort in knowing that the presence and power of Jesus are still with us through the Spirit, there is not much comforting about the way the Spirit works. The Spirit hovers, creates, blows, and explodes upon people throughout the Bible. Images associated with the Holy Spirit are not only the dove but also fire, cloud, and wind. A visit from the Holy Spirit in Scriptures usually means that a character's life is about to change dramatically.

Why is this good news? For people living in similarly tumultuous times, the idea that God is not going to leave us alone is encouraging. If the Bible is right about who God is and how God operates, then the world is infused with the power of transformation and we experience that power through the work of the Holy Spirit. God came into the world in Jesus in order to save it, and the witness to what God was doing then and what God wants to do now is the Holy Spirit.

A WORD FROM THE WRITER

In this book we will explore several ways that the Bible talks about the role of God's Spirit. Though it may seem to be the most insubstantial aspect of God, there is no escaping the Spirit as a major character moving the story of salvation through every part of the Bible. In Chapter 1, we will look at how the Spirit creates and renews from the early days of Creation into our present lives. Chapter 2 lifts up dreams, visions, and the role of trusted mentors in the work of the Spirit to inspire God's people with a new word for a new day. Chapter 3 explores the empowering work of God's Spirit as it plays out in some of the Bible's most colorful figures and in Jesus' ministry. Finally, in Chapter 4, we look at how people have sensed God's continuing presence through the Holy Spirit.

The watchword for this series of studies has been the question, "Why should I care?" How is the story of a spirit, even a holy spirit that moves like wind through human history, supposed to be compelling in a world that considers such thinking magical? For people who have given themselves over to Jesus, however, this talk is not craziness. It is a way of expressing something real about God. They know, as members of those early Celtic Christian communities knew, that there is nothing static about God. God is always on the move, upsetting apple carts and sending ordinary people on to do extraordinary things. The Holy Spirit language helps make sense of how God does this surprising work. Why should you care? Because the Holy Spirit just might be waiting to do the same with you!

As always in these writing enterprises, I am indebted to those who keep me faithful to a calling that is far beyond me. More so than usual in this book I am grateful for my teachers who have helped me understand the work of the Holy Spirit. Eugene Rogers in particular was instrumental in helping me love the study of the Trinity and helping me know why I care about the Holy Spirit.

The people of Franktown United Methodist Church, who know so much about wind and water and the ways the Spirit has moved on our edge of the world, have also provided me with spiritual sustenance and creative challenge that led to this book. The far-flung network of former students I worked with in campus ministry continue to inspire me with their following of the Spirit—journeys I now enjoy sharing through occasional visits and numerous Facebook postings. My family, as always, has encouraged my stories and enriched my days. My children have taught me that parenthood is a grand and glorious adventure. For writing partners and poets who never knew they touched me, I am also thankful.

So here you are on the verge of beginning an exploration into a book on the Holy Spirit. The Spirit is waiting as well to give birth once more to what God will say and do in you. Let's begin!

Alex Joyner

[1]From *Chasing the Wild Goose: The Iona Community,* by Ron Ferguson (Collins, 1988); page 17.

Chapter One

the *Holy Spirit* Creates and Renews

Bible Readings
Genesis 1:1-2; 2:4b-7; Ezekiel 11:19-20; 36:22-26; Joel 2:28-32; Luke 1:26-38; 2:25-38; Acts 2

The Questions
The Bible teaches about the Holy Spirit as One who creates and renews. How can creation and renewal help us understand how God relates to creation and to human beings? What difference can creation and renewal make in our lives?

A Psalm

> O LORD, how manifold are your works!
>
>> In wisdom you have made them all;
>>
>> the earth is full of your creatures.
>
> . . .
>
> When you send forth your spirit, they are created;
>
>> and you renew the face of the ground.
>>
>> Psalm 104:24, 30

A Prayer

Creating and renewing Spirit sent forth from the heart of God, we trust that you know the places in our lives that need to be renewed. You know the ways the world is wounded and how much it cries out for new life. Come, Spirit. Come into this day, into this heart. Amen.

The Power of the Wind

In the coastal region where I live, time is marked as much by the great storms as it is by the passing of seasons and new years. Near my house at a small wharf on a branch of the Chesapeake Bay is a waterman's shed with markings on the blank exterior noting the height of floods since the building was built. The names tell as much about the significant dates in local history as any marker could. Hurricanes such as Donna and Floyd share space with nor'easters such as the infamous 1964 Ash Wednesday storm; and, of course, everyone here knows about the 1933 storm that changed the area forever. It pushed residents off the now-deserted barrier islands and destroyed eel grass in the bays behind them. It altered the fragile ecosystem that provides habitat for scallops, crab, and other staples of the Virginia fishing industry. The winds and the waters of the storms also have a renewing effect here. In the wake of the storms is loss, but there is also rebuilding. New towns emerge, and older communities change. Life begins again. It is no wonder that humans have always felt a mixture of apprehension and awe in the face of wind.

In the Bible the wind is often depicted as a powerful, destructive force. In one story, Elijah, the greatest of Israel's prophets, was called out to a desert mountain where he listened for God in the midst of a violent wind that split the mountain and broke rocks. Along with an accompanying earthquake and fire, the wind was a prelude to God's coming (1 Kings 19:11-13). Even then, when the power of the wind was most obvious, it was a sign of a new day and a new movement of God among the people. The Holy Spirit, the most elusive of the ways God is known in the Bible, is associated with this wind.

When have you had a powerful experience of wind? What feelings did it evoke in you? What might it mean that the Holy Spirit is active in the world like wind?

REFLECT

Creation and Life
Genesis 1:1-2; 2:4b-7
Like wind, the Spirit resists being pinned down, even in pronouns. Is the Spirit a she, a he, an it? All three have been used to refer to the Holy Spirit. Christians consider the Holy Spirit one of the personal names of God but have usually talked in terms of activity rather than gender in describing who the Spirit is. The Spirit blows, moves, breathes, flows, and creates life.

3

According to the Bible, the Holy Spirit was present at the beginning. When the story of who God is gets underway in the opening verses of Genesis, the first description of the cosmos tells us that the Spirit of God was hovering over the waters (Genesis 1:2). The same word that indicates "spirit" can also be translated as "the wind or breath of God." However we imagine it, it is important to note that this is a restless Spirit. There is energy and expectancy in this hovering that soon would be unleashed with creative force. Within a few verses there would be light, stars, planets, and space. The Spirit works across a broad canvas and cannot be contained.

At the end of that first week, however, the focus turned to a more humble creature. Genesis 2 tells a much more intimate story of the creation of a human being from the mud of the earth. To give this new creature life, there was breath once more. God breathed into Adams nostrils the breath of life. Here again, Christians see the Holy Spirit at work.

When I walk through the house at night, I often stop at the doorways of my children's bedrooms. I find great comfort in just hearing them breathe. It is something I have been doing their whole lives. I was fortunate enough to have been there when they both drew their first breath. That was a time of drama because the breath was followed by the great wail of the newborn, but I never took such joy in a crying baby as I did then because I knew it meant this child was drawing in life. Now their nighttime breathing is a gentle affirmation of God's sustaining presence.

In my pastoral ministry, I have also been with persons as they drew their final breath after long lives and long struggles. There is often silence in those rooms, too, as those waiting sit and hold hands and watch each rise and fall of their loved one's chest. The rhythm of those breaths permeates the prayers offered and reminds us of the holiness of the moment. As long as there is breath, there is life.

Recall a time when you were aware of breathing—your own or someone else's. What feelings did that experience inspire in you? If the Holy Spirit entered humanity through breath, how can our breathing continue to signal God's activity in our lives?

REFLECT

A New Spirit
Ezekiel 11:19-20; 36:22-26

When the Creator God rested from labor after six days, it did not mean that the work of creation was over. Genesis gives us the opening scenes of a story that will reveal many acts of creation and renewal. In Ezekiel, we discover that the creating and renewing power of God's Holy Spirit continues.

When the prophet Ezekiel spoke to the people of God, they were in a situation of conflict and crisis. The nation of Israel had been overrun by great powers, and many people had been carried into exile in a distant land. As the people assessed their situation, they began to wonder if their history with God and with the land was finished. Were they being punished for their unfaithfulness? Would others take over Jerusalem? Would God abandon them in their failures?

As Ezekiel listened for God's word in those dark times, he heard clearly that God was going to do a new thing in the people. Even though they had turned away from God and turned toward false gods, God was going to reclaim them. Once again they would be known among the nations as God's own people. More than that, however, God was going to work a change within them. Their hearts, which had turned to stone, were going to be removed in favor of a heart of flesh; and God would put a new spirit within them. Once again we find God intimately connected with these human creatures, breathing in new life. The restless Spirit was on the move again, bringing about renewal.

6

Where are the areas of your life where your heart has become hardened? In what places in your life would you welcome God's Spirit for renewal?

R
E
F
L
E
C
T

Life Is Messy

In the 1989 comedy *Parenthood*, Steve Martin plays Gil Buckman, a harried man who is struggling to look the part of the successful middle-class father while his career and his children are going through crisis. He is not able to experience joy because he worries about so many things, including whether his nine-year-old son will be able to catch a fly ball in a Little League game. His character's moment of grace comes as he is sharing his latest concerns with his patient wife, Karen. "[Our kids are] gonna do a lot of things. Baseball's the least of it. And in all those things, sometimes they're gonna miss." His wife responds by saying, "What do you want? Guarantees? These are kids, not appliances. Life is messy."[1] The way in which his wife responds indicates that there is no messiness in their lives that could overcome a greater love in which all those things take place. There would be problems; but there would always be an adventure, too.

The stories of the Bible testify to the messiness of living in the world and to the disorder in our lives. Time and again God goes back to the people who have fallen and failed and brings about renewal. God seems to know that sometimes we are "gonna miss" and disappoint God and ourselves, but the Holy Spirit works in us to reclaim the original intent for our lives.

What's messy about your life right now? What are the things over which you worry the most? What would change if you were renewed?

R
E
F
L
E
C
T

A New Day Coming
Joel 2:28-32

You want an image for messiness? Try a locust invasion. Joel 2 begins by using the images of conquering armies and devouring locusts to talk about the coming day of the Lord (Joel 2:1-11). In the midst of these dark images, we find a word of hope.

What's in the Bible?
Read Joel 2:28-32. What images are most striking for you in this passage? What does it say to you about the renewing power of God's Spirit? How does Scripture reading offer hope?

A locust swarm was one of the most devastating things that could happen to agricultural communities living on marginal lands. The prophet Joel spoke to a people who knew what locusts could do. Their crops had been devoured by swarms that took away more than the food they needed; they also took away hope. Joel used the darkness of such times to describe a new day when God would come. Joel's vision is cinematic in scope. The sun goes dark, and the moon turns to blood. There is fire and smoke. However, at the heart of the new day is that same renewing spirit that God sends to the people. A day is coming when visions and prophecies of what God wants for creation won't be voiced by a few select people but by everyone. Young and old, slave and free, men and women—all will share in a new community formed by this outpouring of God's Spirit, and any barrier that denied access to God will be torn down.

How do you think Joel's vision of God's renewing Spirit could be a word of hope in our world today?

R E F L E C T

Bible Facts
The term Holy Spirit *is only mentioned in two passages in the Old Testament (Psalm 51:11; Isaiah 63:10-11). Far more frequently the term* spirit *alone is used. The sense of the Holy Spirit as one of the personal names of God becomes clearer in the New Testament. Throughout the Bible when something is referred to as "holy," it indicates being set apart for God's purposes and is fundamentally at odds with sin.*

B I B L E   F A C T S

Overshadowed by the Spirit
Luke 1:26-38; 2:25-38

When Christians refer to the latter books of the Bible as the New Testament, they are not denying the continuing relevance of the Hebrew Scriptures; but they do see God doing something radically new in Jesus. We have seen that it is in the nature of God's Spirit to keep creating and renewing. Now in Luke the same Spirit that hovered in expectancy over the waters comes to overshadow a young woman with the result that she will be expecting a child of promise.

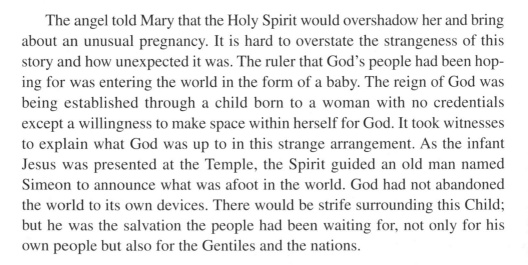

What's in the Bible?
Read Luke 1:26-38; 2:25-38. How does the action of the Holy Spirit in these Scripture passages compare to the action of the Holy Spirit in the previous Scripture passages in this chapter? What does the Spirit's guidance of Simeon tell us about the role of the Spirit?

The angel told Mary that the Holy Spirit would overshadow her and bring about an unusual pregnancy. It is hard to overstate the strangeness of this story and how unexpected it was. The ruler that God's people had been hoping for was entering the world in the form of a baby. The reign of God was being established through a child born to a woman with no credentials except a willingness to make space within herself for God. It took witnesses to explain what God was up to in this strange arrangement. As the infant Jesus was presented at the Temple, the Spirit guided an old man named Simeon to announce what was afoot in the world. God had not abandoned the world to its own devices. There would be strife surrounding this Child; but he was the salvation the people had been waiting for, not only for his own people but also for the Gentiles and the nations.

One of the wonders of the place where I live is the network of large, shallow bays that lie behind the barrier islands. On the Virginia shoreline, the islands arc out from the land, extending out as much as eight miles from the mainland. These bays are fertile waters that provide a nursery for many sea creatures, including fish and sharks. Kayaking here, I often think about what a unique habitat this is. It is almost as if the land opens up to provide space within itself for the flourishing of new life. This is creative space.

Wasn't Mary creating such a space within herself by assenting to the Spirit's movement? Wasn't she offering her very self for the renewal of the world and the advent of a new day? With all of the distractions and busy-ness with which we fill our lives, there is the real danger that we will not have the space for receiving what God has to give. We may also not be open to the new activity of the Holy Spirit that wants to remind us of our purpose and promise.

What is creative space for you that allows you to experience God's presence? How can you create more of it in your life? What might God be calling you to do?

REFLECT

A People Remade
Acts 2

Those who had followed Jesus and had watched the awful and awesome events in Jerusalem as Jesus went from celebrated teacher to crucified criminal to resurrected Savior huddled together in one place at the feast of Pentecost. Jesus had told them all that would happen, but they had trouble understanding what he had meant. More was about to happen.

What's in the Bible?
Read Acts 2. What images or phrases from this passage speak most powerfully to you? What does the gift of the Holy Spirit look like when it is given to the people?

Jesus had promised that when he left them he would send the Holy Spirit upon them. The Spirit would be their companion, their instructor, the one who would help them remember who Jesus was and who they were, and the one who would make Jesus always present with them in a new and vital way. Again they had a hard time accepting what he was saying. So after his departure, they sat together in one place as Jerusalem filled with Jewish pilgrims from around the known world to observe the feast of Pentecost.

Suddenly everything changed. The sound of a violent wind blew through the house. Flames danced above their heads. Just as in the garden of Genesis, the Spirit was breathed into the life of humanity once more and brought about a new day. The Spirit animated this group of expectant disciples and launched them on a journey that would remake the world. At the movement of the Holy Spirit they began to speak in languages that all those foreign visitors could understand, and they told what God could do.

The outburst caused mass confusion, so Peter, a leader of the disciples, stood up to explain. When he did, he recalled the words of the prophet Joel. Hadn't the promise always been that when God came in power the Spirit would be poured out on all people, not just the few and the privileged? Looking around at that ragtag collection of fishermen, tax collectors, and women who lived on the margins, it was clear that this was the promise coming to life in a new community. That day about 3,000 more joined; and the Spirit moved them to a way of living together that emphasized mutual support, shared possessions, and constant attention to God. What would become the church was born.

The Church and the Holy Spirit

The new community that was born in the chaos of that Pentecost outburst was known as the *ecclesia*, a Greek word that simply means "an assembly of people." In English it came to be known as the church. Like any assembly of people, it had its wonders and its flaws. The early ideal of communal living and shared property soon faltered, and the disciples had to grapple with internal divisions and members who struggled to be the holy people they were called to be. In the centuries that have followed, the Christian church has sometimes been at the forefront of great movements, such as the civil rights movement; and it has sometimes supported things that can only be described as evil, such as slavery. The multiplicity of Christian denominations speaks to great diversity among those who follow Jesus, but it also reflects a history of Christian strife.

If you have had experience in Christian churches, what has that been like? How have you seen them as places of renewal? How do they sometimes fail? When have you experienced new life from being part of a gathering of people?

REFLECT

As often as it has failed, however, the church has been reclaimed and renewed by the Holy Spirit. The Bible tells a story of how God continues to come into places where it looks like all energy and life has died and the Holy Spirit blows once more. One of the reasons the church keeps going back to the Bible is to remind itself of how the Holy Spirit has moved through the people of God in the past and of how people just like us kept discovering anew that their lives were part of a bigger story that was going somewhere. The church, empowered by the Holy Spirit, is God's gift to people who need to be renewed and who need the companionship of fellow travelers willing to share their lives with Jesus and with one another.

Here's Why I Care

So what does it mean for you now that the Holy Spirit creates and renews? Are there places crying out for a fresh wind? Where do you see the Holy Spirit at work in the world and in your life bringing about a new day? What can you do to cooperate with what the Holy Spirit wants to do in you?

A Prayer

Holy Spirit, we trust that you are hovering just above our heads in expectation of doing a new thing. We trust that you are waiting to fill us with life as you have done with all creation. We trust that you will renew and empower us; in Christ we pray. Amen.

---

[1]From the script for *Parenthood* at *script-o-rama.com/movie_scripts/p/parenthood-script-transcript-steve-martin.html*.

Chapter Two

the *Holy Spirit*
Inspires

Bible Readings
Genesis 41; 2 Kings 2:1-15; Isaiah 48:12-19; Zechariah 7:8-14; Luke 1:39-45, 57-80; 4:16-21

The Questions
The Bible teaches about the Holy Spirit as One who inspires people with the knowledge of God's will and ways. How can the inspiration of the Holy Spirit help us understand how God wants us to live as God's people? What difference can the inspiration of the Holy Spirit make in our lives?

_____

_____

_____

_____

_____

_____

_____

_____

_____

_____

A Psalm

Teach me to do your will,

for you are my God.

Let your good spirit lead me on a level path.

Psalm 143:10

A Prayer

God, sometimes the deepest jungle is in my very soul. I wander in search of the way that will lead me to you and to my truest self. Inspire me with the wisdom of your Spirit so that I can walk in confidence with you. Amen.

Terrain of Uncertainty

I could see it in their eyes. When I was a campus minister, I began to notice it in the students I worked with as they entered their final year of school. The world was about to change for them. They were gifted students who had received a great education. At graduation exercises they would be told that they could now do anything they wanted; but in their eyes I often saw the question—What is it that I want to do? I recognize the look because I had been there. My college years were a time of great discovery for me when I learned that I could do things I didn't know that I could do. I enjoyed exploring different classes, from Chinese history to folklore studies. I helped run the student radio station. Then graduation loomed, and I had to face a new question. With all the things that I *could* do, what *should* I do? The practical question was, "Where am I going to get a job?" but the bigger question was, "What is God calling me to do with my life?"

As I walked with many students through the struggles of vocational discernment, I got to know that terrain of uncertainty all over again. There were questions about the economy and whether there would be jobs available. There were questions of competence as students wondered if they had what they needed to succeed; but the questions of the soul were the deepest. Some felt called by the needs of the world to go out in service. Others were motivated by a quest, a sense of inner purpose. When these soul concerns connected with a vision of where God was calling them to go, it was always a

18

powerful moment. Such moments can also be thought of as moments when we are inspired by God's Holy Spirit.

Have you ever felt uncertain about what to do with your life? What was it like? How was God present for you?

Joseph, Dreams, and God's Spirit
Genesis 41

The Bible has several stories about the way God's Spirit inspires people through dreams. One such story is that of Joseph in Genesis 41.

What's in the Bible?
Read Genesis 41. What stands out for you about Joseph's response to Pharaoh? What must Pharaoh have seen in him to say that he had God's Spirit?

19

Interpreting dreams caused trouble for Joseph when he was growing up. Back in Canaan he had been the one having the dreams; and when he shared them with his brothers, it made them angry. He was his father's favorite, the one Jacob spared from hard labor and outfitted with a special coat. Jacob loved him more than the others, and the brothers could tell. So when Joseph shared his dream about the brother's sheaves of wheat bowing down to his sheaf of wheat, they had no doubt what the dream meant; and they didn't like it. Later, when he told of a dream in which the sun, moon, and 11 stars were bowing down to him, Joseph's 11 brothers drew their own conclusions again and began plotting his undoing (Genesis 37:1-11).

Their opportunity came one day when they were far out in the wilderness watching the flocks. Joseph showed up on a mission from his father. As the dreamer walked toward them, they conspired to kill him. "Let's see what becomes of his dreams then!" they said to one another. In the end, the arrival of a slave trader led them to change their plans from murder; and they sold Joseph into slavery in Egypt (37:12-36). They thought this would bring an end to his dreams. Joseph would not be the one to whom others would bow down; he would do the bowing.

Joseph's lot grew worse in Egypt. He ended up in prison where he was a cellmate with two former servants of the pharaoh, Egypt's powerful king. When they both had vivid dreams, Joseph correctly interpreted them; but even though he asked the man who was restored as the pharaoh's cupbearer to remember him when he was released from prison, the man did not (Chapter 40). Joseph remained in prison until the pharaoh had a troubling dream that no one seemed to be able to interpret. Then the cupbearer remembered his cellmate and his remarkable facility with dreams. Joseph was released and brought before Pharaoh. He was able to interpret the dream, and in his gratitude Pharaoh made Joseph second-in-command to oversee preparations for the famine that Joseph had foreseen in the dream. It seemed that Joseph's original dreams were coming true after all. People were bowing down to him. Soon his brothers would come to Egypt and bow before him, too.

Something was happening with Joseph, though. At the very moment of his elevation, he was beginning to give credit to someone besides himself. He claimed that it was God who was giving him the insight and wisdom to understand what was going on (41:16). For his part, Pharaoh was able to see that Joseph was filled with the Spirit of God (verse 38); and that gave him the discernment he needed to lead the people through a time of crisis.

There are lots of theories about dreams and what they mean. In Genesis, the dreams of Joseph, his cellmates, and Pharaoh were prophetic, indicating what would happen in the future. Other biblical dreams are occasions for God to communicate more directly, often through angels, with people such as Abraham; Jacob; Paul; and another Joseph, Jesus' father. Today we are more likely to think of dreams as symbolic ways that our brains sort out the many things that happen each day. In the age after psychologists such as Sigmund Freud and Carl Jung, we recognize the power of our subconscious minds.

Dreams are an ancient source of inspiration in most cultures. Many people claim that they don't remember their dreams, but I suspect that is due to our reluctance to give much weight to them. In recent years I have tried to be more mindful of my dreams, even praying that God will give me one for insight. I keep paper and pen near my bed to scribble down those elusive images that would otherwise disappear beneath the weight of more mundane concerns. There are things I have learned about myself that I would not have known had I not been listening for God's Spirit speaking in the night.

What do you believe dreams can tell us? How might God speak through them? When has a dream inspired you to make a change in your life?

REFLECT

The Prophets and God's Spirit
Isaiah 48:12-19; Zechariah 7:8-14

In later years, after Israel had become a nation, God's Spirit inspired and spoke through the prophets who interpreted for the people what God intended to do and what God called them to do. The prophets were inspired agents, given new eyes to see what was going on around them. They often lived difficult lives, struggling with God because of the hard things they had to share with the people and struggling with the people because of their resistance to what they had to say. It was a lonely life but one in which they could never assume that God was not speaking. The fire within them told them that God's Spirit was there, moving them to a holy mission. In Isaiah 48:12-19 and Zechariah 7:8-14, the Spirit of God speaks through the prophets to the people known by the name of their ancestor Jacob, who was also called Israel.

What's in the Bible?
Read Isaiah 48:12-19 and Zechariah 7:8-14. What stands out for you in these Scripture passages? What is God's great desire for the people in these Scriptures? How are the Scriptures similar? How are they different?

Isaiah 48:12-19 addresses the people of Israel after they were taken into exile in Babylon, an event that might not have happened had they only listened to God and lived according to God's guidance. God's Spirit inspired the prophet to remind them what God had done for them in the past and that God continued to speak to them. God's Spirit remained with them. The prophet called them to "draw near and hear this!" God's Spirit does not speak in secret. Even though God had been present since Creation, revealing the things they should do, the people neglected to listen. Inspired by the Spirit, Isaiah called the people to remember that God taught them and led them for their own good.

The theme of refusing to listen shows up again in Zechariah 7:8-14. The words of this passage are addressed to the people of Israel after the Exile. They remind the people of the consequences of not listening to and heeding God's words. As God's people, they were called to live God's way. Inspired by God's Spirit, the prophet reminded them, "Render true judgments, show kindness and mercy to one another; do not oppress the widow, the orphan, the alien, or the poor; and do not devise evil in your hearts against one another" (verses 9-10). As in Isaiah, the people refused to listen to the words sent by God's Spirit through the prophets (verse 12). The prophet reminded them of the consequences of not listening to the Spirit of God through the prophets in the past: The people were defeated, exiled, and scattered.

What do you think the prophets would say to us today? How might God's Spirit inspire us if we listened to them? What difference could it make?

REFLECT

Mentors, Leaders, and God's Spirit
2 Kings 2:1-15

We met Elijah once before in this book. In Session 1, he was the prophet on a desert mountain listening for God in the midst of howling winds and shattered rocks. There was always something dramatic about this prophet, so it is not surprising that his final scene involved a whirlwind, too.

What's in the Bible?

Read 2 Kings 2:1-15. What challenges you or makes you curious about this Scripture? What details capture your imagination? What hopes might Elisha have in requesting a double portion of the Spirit? How do you see God's Spirit at work in the relationship between Elijah and Elisha?

Through the course of his prophetic ministry, Elijah had acquired a reputation and a faithful disciple, Elisha, whom he seems to have tested on their journey to the Jordan. At each stage of the trip, Elijah told the younger prophet to stay in place while he journeyed on. Each time, Elisha refused to listen and insisted on accompanying the older man. Along the way, groups of prophets warned Elisha that God was going to take his master away that day. Elisha's response was simple: "I know."

A clear sense of change was in the air as the two men made their way to the river. Many years before, the people of Israel had walked this same passage. Back then, Joshua, taking up the work of Moses in leading the people, led them through the Jordan as it parted for them to cross into the land God had promised them. Now the river parted again as Elijah rolled up his mantle and struck the waters. The two men crossed to the other side, and Elisha made his final request of his mentor.

Elisha knew that what gave Elijah his power and his role among the people was his ability to hear God clearly and to interpret God's will to the nation. As we know, this was the role of the Spirit; and this is what Elisha asked of the prophet. It was the tradition in this society for the first-born to inherit a double portion of the property of the father. Though Elijah was not Elisha's father, the relationship was similar; and so Elisha asked for a double portion of the Spirit so that he could be Elijah's true heir.

Bible Facts

Jewish people reading this story would have heard echoes of the account of the people of Israel entering the Promised Land. Second Kings 2:8 evokes memories of Moses parting the seas (Exodus 15:14-21). Moses handed over leadership to Joshua on the east bank of the Jordan, where Elisha picked up the mantle of Elijah. The story from Second Kings shows that Elijah and Elisha stand in the tradition of those who led God's people in the past.

BIBLE FACTS

When I was a teenager, I was fortunate to have an Elijah in my life. A young pastor named Brooke Willson had become the director of youth ministries for the churches in our area; and over the course of several years, we traveled to many youth events together. Those experiences were so vivid for me that I even remember the Volkswagen Rabbit that he drove, the one with the floor mat on the passenger side with the final T worn off so that it read "Rabbi."

Even more important in my memory are the conversations we had as we traveled. The Rev. Willson was nothing if not passionate, railing against the injustices in the world and the church with the vigor of an Old Testament prophet. Whether the subject was bishops or theology or the death penalty, I could count on a lively conversation. Sometimes I found his words attractive, sometimes scary, sometimes wrong, but always fascinating. He spoke with a clarity I desired in my life. During a time when I was just developing my sense of what God wanted for me and for the world, he acted as a spiritual provocateur, spurring me on to new stages of development.

I recognize now that I received an inheritance of a sort from this mentor. As I walked with him, I was able to hear God calling me. As my vocation developed, it was different from his; but it was the same Spirit that inspired both of us. In the midst of all the voices competing for my adolescent attention, that spirit helped me discern something I could call truth.

Who has acted as an Elijah in your life, provoking you to new understandings of who you are? Who acts as a mentor for you now? How can she or he help you listen for God's Spirit?

R E F L E C T

An Elderly Couple and the Holy Spirit
Luke 1:39-45, 57-80

The tradition of prophets being inspired by God's Spirit to speak a new word for a new day continues in the stories of Jesus. In the last session, we looked at the new thing that the Holy Spirit brought about for Mary as she was told that she would have a child. Surrounding that episode in the Book of Luke is the story of an elderly couple who had their own encounter with the Spirit.

What's in the Bible?
Read Luke 1:39-45, 57-80. How do you respond to Elizabeth's exclamation in verses 39-45? What details reveal the connections between the Holy Spirit and new life? How do you respond to Zechariah's prophecy? What do the Spirit-inspired prophecies of Elizabeth and Zechariah say to you about the work of the Holy Spirit?

Elizabeth and Zechariah had long been following God. Zechariah was a priest, and he and Elizabeth were faithful; but they had not had any children, which was sometimes taken as a sign of God's rejection in their society. In their later years, however, God blessed Zechariah and Elizabeth with the birth of a child. When Zechariah first received the news of the pregnancy from Gabriel in the Temple, he did not believe it; and he was struck dumb until the child was born and named.

When they did find their voices, these two new parents had a new role. They were filled with the Holy Spirit, and they were inspired to tell the world what God was doing with a new round of unexpected pregnancies. When Mary came to visit, Elizabeth felt her child leap within her; and she knew that God was bringing some great thing to birth through her young relative. She shouted out that Mary was the mother of the Lord—an extraordinary thing to say about someone of her lowly status. Zechariah got to deliver the proclamation about their own child, whom they named John. Filled with the Spirit, the old priest shared his vision that John would be the one who would go ahead of Jesus, preparing the people for the dawning of a time of hope and light.

When have you had an overwhelming sense of something good about to happen in your life? What was it like?

REFLECT

The Scriptures and the Spirit of the Lord
Luke 4:16-21

Jesus stood in the Temple, and inspired by God's Spirit, he read and interpreted the words of a prophet named Isaiah. He proclaimed his ministry as a fulfillment of Isaiah's words.

What's in the Bible?
Read Luke 4:16-21. How do you respond to Jesus' reading from the prophet Isaiah? What challenges you or appeals to you? What do you think about Jesus using the words of a Scripture reading to communicate the inspiration of God's Spirit?

When Jesus stood to read the Scriptures in the synagogue that day, there were some who had a hard time hearing the words he was saying. He was in Nazareth, his childhood home; and the listeners were people who knew his family. The prophecies of Elizabeth and Zechariah had not resonated here. To these people, Jesus was Joseph's boy. They had seen him in all the awkward stages of his development. They knew this young man, or at least they thought they did. It was hard to hear the words because they were so taken with the person who was reading them, but the words were important. Originally they had been spoken by Isaiah who was proclaiming a new day for the people of Israel. The Spirit of the Lord had come to the prophet to tell the people that a new order was going to be established in which those on the outside of society would be brought to the center. The poor, the blind, the oppressed, the captives—these were the ones who would receive the good news.

Now, however, Jesus was bringing these words to new life. As he sat down in a teaching position before the assembly, he made it clear: "Today this Scripture has been fulfilled in your hearing" (Luke 4:21). Suddenly Jesus was not just reading ancient history. Inspired by God's Spirit, he was ushering in a new age. The effect was so dramatic that it shocked those who assumed they knew what they were hearing and seeing.

One of the ways that Christians have understood the work of the Holy Spirit is as interpreter. It might seem a strange thing that an ancient book like the Bible is read each week in churches and by individuals throughout the world. What could a book filled with the histories of people and cultures long since passed say for contemporary situations? Often, before reading the Scriptures in a church service, there will be a prayer of illumination, inviting the Holy Spirit to come into the act of reading to speak a fresh word from God. In this way the Bible becomes a living document, inspired with a living word.

Recently, I ran across an old journal full of my thoughts and newspapers clippings from my youth. The words and articles there were obviously important to me at the time. Reading them again at my current age, they mean something different. I hear things about my family and friends and my developing identity that I could not have heard then, but it was all there in the words. Going back to them again I find a new message; it is the same with the Bible. Because Christians believe that the Holy Spirit was involved in the writing of these words, we also know that there is something alive here.

What new words have you heard as you have read the Bible? What did you expect to hear when you began this study? If you expected the Holy Spirit to speak to you through the Bible, what would change about how you read it?

REFLECT

Listen to the Spirit of God

Dreams, visions, journeys with trusted elders, reading Scriptures—we have seen the Holy Spirit working through all of these as we have explored these Bible passages. Joseph, the prophets, Elijah, Elisha, Elizabeth, and Zechariah are not just names in a book; they are our fellow travelers, still filled with the Spirit and still speaking to us. The Holy Spirit inspired them, inspired Jesus, and continues to inspire us today if we listen.

Here's Why I Care
What can you do to welcome the Holy Spirit in for inspiration?
What is one thing you can do to be more attuned to the ways the
Spirit is seeking to speak to you?

A Prayer

Spirit of truth, I give you thanks that you have chosen many ways to speak in my life. Help me be open to how you speak and where you lead. With all the voices calling out for my attention, let the one I hear be yours. Amen.

Chapter Three

the Holy Spirit
Empowers

Bible Readings

Judges 14–15; 1 Samuel 11:1-15; 16; Matthew 12:15-21; Luke 3:15-22; 4:1-14; Acts 10:34-38

The Questions

The Bible teaches about the Holy Spirit as One who empowers God's people with the courage, strength, and ability to do God's will. How can the empowering activity of the Holy Spirit help us as we seek to know and to do God's will? What difference can the power of the Holy Spirit make in our lives?

_____

_____

_____

_____

_____

_____

_____

_____

_____

_____

_____

A Psalm

> Create in me a clean heart, O God,
>
> > and put a new and right spirit within me.
>
> Do not cast me away from your presence,
>
> > and do not take your holy spirit from me.
> >
> > Psalm 51:10-11

A Prayer

Empowering Spirit of God, in the face of great challenges I often wonder if I am able to do what you want me to do. I know my limitations, but you know my potential. Come and meet me in my weakness, and give me strength—your strength. Amen.

Superheroes at the Multiplex

We rarely go to the multiplex movie theaters these days without seeing a movie about somebody in spandex. One of the most successful formulas for moviemaking now are films that feature a flawed or troubled central character blessed and burdened with super powers that he or she uses for some grand, heroic act of justice against fantastic villains. For some reason, the uniform of choice for these characters is usually spandex. Dress choice aside, the attraction of these movies is that they offer us fantasies of what we could do if only we were such powerful people. After all, we know injustice when we see it. We know that there are dark forces lurking out there, waiting to do harm to our loved ones and to us. We know that if we just had superhuman strength or could fly or become invisible, we would use those powers to set things right. Even a few cool, technological gadgets would help!

The longing for power is a common human desire. When we feel disempowered, we are vulnerable to despair, depression, anger, bitterness, and physical illness. However, we are also aware of the dangers of power. Lord Acton may be credited with the saying, but we would know the truth of it even if he hadn't coined it: "Power tends to corrupt and absolute power corrupts absolutely."[1] In one way or another, every movie superhero struggles with this truism.

The Strength of Samson
Judges 14–15

The Bible offers us its own collection of flawed heroes. Even men and women who are held up as models of strength and faithfulness are often revealed to have major weaknesses. This is never more apparent than in the story of Samson.

What's in the Bible?
Read Judges 14–15. What challenges you in this story? What appeals to you? Why? What is attractive about Samson and his strength? Where is God in this story?

Samson is one of the larger-than-life characters we run into in the Book of Judges. He is a superhero during a time when the Philistines ruled over the Israelites. The story begins in Judges 13 with a visit from the angel of the Lord to the barren wife of Manoah. The angel promised that they would have a son and instructed that they should raise the son as a nazirite, one who was dedicated to the service of the Lord. The angel also said, "It is he who shall begin to deliver Israel from the hand of the Philistines" (13:5). Samson grew up to be a powerful man who could stand up to their enemies. He could tear apart lions with his bare hands and slay those who opposed him armed only with a donkey's jawbone.

Samson was deeply flawed, however. He was ruled by his senses rather than by his logic. He was also impulsive and prone to fits of jealous rage. When Samson saw something or someone he wanted, he showed no restraint in getting it. These qualities of character caused harm to the Philistine women that he married, to their families, and to the Israelites. So it might be surprising to see God's Spirit show up in the midst of his story. At key moments in Samson's life, the Spirit rushed upon him to enable him to perform spectacular acts, which to us seem excessive but were somehow working out a larger purpose in God's eyes (14:6, 19). The source of Samson's strength was the Spirit of the Lord.

It is perhaps best to see Samson in the same way that we look at those superheroes of the cinema. It would be great to have their power to take on the "bad guys" that stand against us; but we also know that they, and we, have to deal with our hearts as well. Who wouldn't want to have Samson's strength, but wouldn't we also struggle with what to do with it? The larger message is the message of God's presence and the power of God's Spirit with the oppressed Israelites and with their deeply flawed hero.

When have you felt that you didn't have the power to face something threatening in your life? If God's Spirit "rushed on you" to empower you to confront something you need to deal with, what would it be?

REFLECT

Bible Facts
The term judge, *which is used throughout the Book of Judges, means more than "one who handles legal disputes." Judges were leaders who had local authority to govern the people and who often served as military leaders to deliver the Israelites from enemies. Samson was a judge for 20 years (Judges 15:20).*

BIBLE FACTS

God's Spirit and a King
1 Samuel 11:1-15

The closing chapters of the Book of Judges paint a picture of a collapsing society. A loosely unified Israel and the tribal structure they lived with meant that they were sometimes fighting not only external enemies but also one anther. The Book of First Samuel documents the movement of the people toward a new political structure headed by a king.

What's in the Bible?

Read 1 Samuel 11:1-15. What images jump out at you from this passage? What challenges you or appeals to you? How is the power of God's Spirit at work in this story?

God's Spirit has a key role in this story of how Saul became king. As in the story of Samson, the Spirit of God is the source of power and strength. The story begins with a threat from the Ammonites. Saul was incensed by the demand that in order to enter a treaty with the Ammonites, everyone's right eye must be gouged out. "And the spirit of God came upon Saul in power when he heard these words" (1 Samuel 11:6). Saul was spurred into military action that saved the people from disgrace. As a result, Saul became king.

The path to being ruled by a king was not simple or easy. While the people wanted strength and unity to fight off foes, there was at least one man who knew the dangers of handing over power to a single ruler. Samuel was a prophet who had been called by God as a boy at a time when "the word of the LORD was rare" (3:1). He struggled with the people, trying to help them see that there was no substitute for following God. He warned Israel that a king would inevitably take things that were dear to them—their sons for armies, their daughters for servants, their land and their wealth for his own use (8:10-20). However, the people were insistent; and after Saul proved himself in a conflict with the Ammonites, they settled into life with a king. The source of power for the warrior-king was God's Spirit.

Have you ever become angry because of an injustice? What was it like? Were you able to do anything? How do you think the power of God's Spirit might be at work in such situations?

R E F L E C T

A Shepherd Becomes King
1 Samuel 16

In First Samuel, we see God's Spirit in an additional role in the work of the kings. God's Spirit still came upon the king to empower him to do great deeds, as we see in the story of Saul and the Ammonites; but the Spirit was also a sign of God's election of the king to represent the people. If the king and the people listened and followed God, the Spirit would give them strength. If the king and the people did not listen to God's commands, then God's hand would be against them.

Saul's story doesn't have a happy ending. He was a troubled hero dealing with difficult times, and inevitably he ran up against Samuel's warnings. Caught in an act of disobedience, suddenly he found that God had turned against him (1 Samuel 15). The people had become used to doing what was right in their own eyes, and now God was insisting on another standard. The king bore the weight of God's high expectations, and he lost God's favor and Spirit.

In secret, Samuel set out on another mission. This time God sent the prophet to visit a family in Bethlehem, where he was told he would find the new king. Jesse had many fine-looking sons who looked the part; but after visiting seven of them, Samuel had still not found the one whom God had chosen. God gave the standard for who would be empowered to serve as king in 1 Samuel 16:7: "The LORD said to Samuel, 'Do not look on his appearance or on the height of his stature . . . for the LORD does not see as mortals see; they look on the outward appearance, but the LORD looks on the heart.' " Seven of Jesse's sons were brought before Samuel, and none of them were chosen. Finally the youngest boy, David, was brought in from the fields, where he had been watching the sheep. David may not have had the stature of his older brothers, but he was a handsome fellow with beautiful eyes. God told Samuel that David was the one he had come for; and in the presence of his brothers, Samuel anointed David. Those watching must have known the significance of this action. The greatest holy man in the nation was pouring oil on the head of a young man. David was destined for leadership.

The Bible underscores what was going on. It tells us that God's Spirit came on David at that moment. Almost immediately it tells us that the Spirit departed from Saul. A transfer of power was taking place, though it would take many more small dramas before it was recognized in fact. David would rise to become the greatest of Israel's rulers, though he would also prove to be a man of outsized flaws.

Saul would begin a slow decline. Troublingly, an evil spirit from God afflicted Saul. He experienced a form of mental distress that could only be alleviated by music. He asked for a skilled musician to play for him, and a servant suggested a young man with qualifications far beyond what was called for. He was not only a master of the lyre, but a warrior, well-spoken, and of good character. It was only a knife in Saul's wound when the servant added that "the LORD is with him," as if to say, "God is obviously no longer with you." That young man turned out to be the very person Samuel had anointed to take Saul's place. David took up residence in Saul's court; and when he played, the evil spirit from God would depart. However, the Spirit that would empower a leader for God's people was no longer with Saul. David was the representative of the people now. God's Spirit was with him.

However, after rising to become king, David displayed his own imperfections by taking another man's wife as his own and arranging for her husband's death (2 Samuel 11–12). The psalm at the beginning of this chapter is part of a song of remorse attributed to David as he sought God's forgiveness for what he had done in that incident.

In an age influenced by the psychoanalytic theories of Sigmund Freud, we have come to expect that all people, even people of great character, sometimes act out of base motives of which they are not even consciously aware. When a politician is caught in a compromising position or a religious leader falls from grace because of money or sex, we are disappointed but not entirely surprised. It is a truth as old as the Bible that leaders will let us down from time to time. They will not live up to their highest ideals or God's desires for them.

So what do we make of these stories of God's Spirit moving through these human characters we have been reading about? The Bible invites us into these rich and earthy narratives, not so that we can be shocked at the bad behavior we find there but so that we can be amazed at what God can do with even characters such as Samson, Saul, and David. When the Spirit came on these people, they were given the courage and capacity to do astounding things. If they could be empowered for service, maybe God could do the same with people like us. True leadership is marked by the power and presence of God's Spirit.

What connections do you make in the story of God's power in Saul and David to political situations in our contemporary culture? How do you see God's power at work in those who lead?

REFLECT

Jesus Empowered for Ministry
Luke 3:15-22

God's Spirit came on the judges and the kings so that they could act on behalf of God's people. When they were empowered by the Spirit, these human agents were able to rise above their character flaws and other challenges. The power of God's Holy Spirit is an important dimension of the life and ministry of Jesus as well.

What's in the Bible?
Read Luke 3:15-22. What images strike you in this passage? What does this Scripture say to you about the empowering work of the Holy Spirit? How is the empowering work of the Holy Spirit in this Scripture similar to the previous Scriptures in this chapter?

Unlike the flawed heroes we have been looking at, Jesus is not only human but divine. He reveals the nature of God and God's vision of what human beings can be. In his life, death, and resurrection, he represents us— all those who struggle to be more fully human and more holy.

John the Baptist, whom we saw in the last chapter at his birth, certainly had an elevated sense of who Jesus was. When he appeared at the Jordan River, he began to prepare those who came to see him for the coming of one whose sandals he would not be worthy to tie. He baptized others; but the Gospel of Matthew tells us that when Jesus came to him, John balked at the idea that Jesus would need baptism (Matthew 3:14). Though Jesus was coming to do a new thing, he stood in the same tradition as Elijah and Elisha who went through this same Jordan River. In all three Gospel accounts of Jesus' baptism, the Holy Spirit descended upon him and empowered him for the work he had to do. A proclamation of Jesus' identity came in a voice from heaven: "You are my Son, the Beloved; with you I am well pleased" (Mark 1:11; also Psalm 2:7; Isaiah 42:1; and Matthew 3:17). The ministry of Jesus begins.

What differences do you see in the empowering work of the Holy Spirit at Jesus' baptism and in the previous stories of Samson, Saul, and David?

REFLECT

Strength Through Temptation
Luke 4:1-14

Right after his baptism and at the beginning of his public ministry, Jesus was led by the Spirit into the wilderness, where he would encounter a series of temptations.

What's in the Bible?
Read Luke 4:1-14. How do you respond to this encounter between Jesus and the devil? What challenges do you see for Jesus in the temptations the devil offered? What insights do you gain from Jesus' responses?

Jesus went into the wilderness filled with the Holy Spirit and led by the Spirit. When Jesus spent 40 days in the wilderness, it echoed the journey of the people of Israel who had wandered in the wilderness for 40 years. Just as Moses needed the strength of God's power to lead the people through the wilderness where they would be shaped into the people of God, Jesus needed the strength that the Spirit provided in order to sort through what his ministry would mean. Some people expected a messiah who would be a warrior-king like David and re-establish Israel. What would it mean to live and lead as the Son of God? In the midst of his retreat to the desert, the devil showed up to tempt him. Jesus countered every temptation to misuse the power given to him by God.

We might say that some of the characters we have looked at above were fighting their own demons, to speak metaphorically. God's Spirit helped those Old Testament figures fight off foes. As then, the power of the Spirit allowed Jesus to turn back the tempter and to confirm his identity in what God intended. He left the wilderness filled with that power, and word began to spread. "Something new is happening here," they must have said. "Watch him."

Temptations distract us from being what we are meant to be in God's eyes. With what are you being tempted right now? If Jesus is our model for how to respond to temptations, what can you learn from Jesus about strategies for dealing with them? What role can the Holy Spirit play?

R E F L E C T

Power to Serve
Matthew12:15-21; Acts 10:34-38

Jesus' ministry marked him as a different kind of king than Saul or David. The Holy Spirit was empowering him, not for violent conflict or political rule but for service.

What's in the Bible?
Read Matthew 12:15-21 and Acts 10:34-38. What images stand out for you in these readings? What did the Holy Spirit empower Jesus to do? What is different about the kind of power the Holy Spirit gives here than the kind of power displayed by Samson, Saul, and David? What does the Scripture say to you about changes in the way God's people understood the power of God's Spirit over the centuries?

Matthew 12 quotes Isaiah 42:1-4, 9, which presents an image of a chosen and beloved servant empowered by God's Spirit for justice for all people, including Gentiles. Peter's sermon in Acts 10:34-38 echoes the same understanding of what the Holy Spirit empowered Jesus as "Lord of all" to do. "God anointed Jesus of Nazareth with the Holy Spirit and with power . . . he went about doing good and healing all who were oppressed" (Acts 10:38). The old prophecies were heard in a new light because of the way Jesus moved among the people. He stopped to be with people who were on the margins. He healed sick people. He welcomed outcasts. He challenged his own people with the radical notion that God's love was meant for everyone. For people who had always seen Gentiles as outside of God's concern, the idea that they were suddenly heirs to the good news of God was a test; but the Spirit was opening up a new day. When Peter talked about Jesus in preaching, he would sound a little like the servant announcing the new day of David to troubled Saul: "God was with him" (Acts 10:38).

How do you see the Holy Spirit empowering people to serve? Who among your friends or acquaintances comes to mind? Why? How do they serve?

REFLECT

A Boost From the Holy Spirit

One of my friends runs a nearby church camp. Recently the camp installed a climbing wall, and Jerry spends a lot of his summer anchoring the rope for youth who make their way carefully up the 30-foot ascent. Sometimes, and always unobtrusively, Jerry will give the climber a little additional lift to reach the next handhold. By leaning backward from his position on the ground, he can provide a boost that is not always noticed.

When a child reaches the top for the first time, they may not know to give some of the credit to the man on the other end of the rope; but the effect is noticeable. They have gone somewhere new, and they now have confidence to go other places. I like to think the Holy Spirit sometimes works like Jerry on the climbing wall. Even though we may be unaware of the power of the Holy Spirit at work in our lives, we can count on God to give us a boost, to give us confidence and power for our lives.

Here's Why I Care

The Holy Spirit moves through the stories of the Bible with power, enabling people to do the things God calls them to do. What does that mean for us? for you? Where are the places in your life that are crying out for courage to bring about something new? Who would the Holy Spirit empower you to serve?

HERE'S WHY I CARE

A Prayer

Holy Spirit, you know that we are not superheroes. We long for more power, yet we misuse the power we have. Come and fill us with the courage we need to serve you and the world. We trust that you can use us and pray that you will. Amen.

---

[1]From *quotes.liberty-tree.ca/quotes_by/lord+acton.*

Chapter Four

the Holy Spirit
Is With God's People

Bible Readings
*Isaiah 32:14-17; 59:20-21; Matthew 28:19-20; Luke 10:21-22; 11:1-13;
24:44-49; John 14:15-27; 16:12-15; Acts 6; 2 Corinthians 3:4-18;
Galatians 5:16-25*

The Questions
The Bible teaches about the Holy Spirit as One whose creating, inspiring,
and empowering activity remains with God's people. How can we recognize
the activity of the Holy Spirit in the church and in our individual lives? What
difference can it make to trust the presence of the Holy Spirit with us?

A Psalm

Where can I go from your spirit?

Or where can I flee from your presence?

If I ascend to heaven, you are there;

if I make my bed in Sheol, you are there.

If I take the wings of the morning

and settle at the farthest limits of the sea,

even there your hand shall lead me,

and your right hand shall hold me fast.

Psalm 139:7-10

A Prayer

Pursuing Spirit, you know how often I try to do it alone and how many times I have felt far from you. You are always with me, though, and you do not rest until you claim me. Remind me that I am not alone, and open me to what you will do anew in me and in your church. Amen.

Walking Alone

It was late on a summer night when I saw him. He was walking through a half-circle of light shining down from the streetlamp overhead. As I turned the dilapidated van down the street to follow him, he disappeared into a patch of darkness. It was Vergie, a 12-year-old boy I had been working with for several months. I was in the middle of my internship year at seminary in Dallas. One of my roles in that year was as the youth director of a church-related community center in the inner city. Many afternoons and evenings I spent picking up at-risk youth for the basketball team we had started. On this night, I had just dropped off the last of the team when I saw Vergie.

I stopped the van and got out. Though I knew most of the houses on this street were occupied, it felt like an abandoned town. I followed Vergie through the dappled light on the sidewalk until he was just ahead of me.

"We missed you at practice, Vergie." No response. "Where are you going?" Vergie kept walking. "Can I give you a ride home?"

"I can't go home. My mom doesn't want me there."

"I don't believe that. Let's go see."

His eyes were wet with tears when he finally turned around to walk back to the van with me. I really didn't believe it. How could a mother reject her own child? I knew that she had some issues of substance abuse and mental illness. I knew Vergie had been in trouble with the law, minor acting-out things, sometimes defending his mother when other kids mocked her; but I just couldn't fathom that Vergie would feel safer on the streets than at home.

The house was a few blocks away. We walked up on the darkened porch, me in the lead with Vergie just behind. I spoke to his mother through a small crack she opened in the door. She said, yes, Vergie could come home; but then she saw him moving further into my shadow. Immediately she flew into a rage that spoke volumes of the pain and brokenness in the home. Vergie left with me and eventually ended up in the detention center. When I talked with his probation officer about his case, he told me, "Oh, yes. Vergie. We call kids like him 'throwaways.' "

You and I know that there are too many throwaways in the world, people who feel that their only option is to walk alone because every other message they receive is that they are worthless and undesirable. Maybe you have been there yourself. There are plenty of dark streets to wander down wondering if you'll ever be accepted at home.

What situations have you encountered that are similar to Vergie's? Have you ever felt as though you were a "throwaway"? What was it like?

REFLECT

The Restoring Spirit
Isaiah 32:14-17; 59:20-21

The Bible's story is one of people finding their life and their home. As the psalm affirms, God's Spirit does not leave us alone. If we walk away, the Holy Spirit chases us to the ends of the earth to remind us of who we are meant to be. The Spirit also restores what is lost and wounded and promises a new day.

What's in the Bible?
Read Isaiah 32:14-17; 59:20-21. What images, words, or phrases in this passage offer hope? Why? How might the images of the abandoned city and the fruitful field speak to a people who had lost everything?

In the Old Testament we see God speaking through the prophets over and over again, urging the people to turn around and accept God's Spirit and way of life. As long as they kept walking away from God, they would experience brokenness; but there was hope for them and for the nation if they stopped walking alone. The promises of Isaiah 32:14-17 spoke to a people who were at risk of being conquered by Assyria. In the midst of the wilderness, Isaiah promised a fruitful field, justice, righteousness, and peace. Isaiah 59 speaks of the continuing presence of God's Spirit, not only at the moment but forever.

Sending the Advocate
John 14:15-27; 16:12-15

Jesus was concerned that his disciples not see themselves as walking alone either. As he prepared his followers for the day when he would no longer physically be present with them, he began to speak about the Holy Spirit.

As in the days when God's Spirit spoke through the prophets, Jesus told the disciples that the Holy Spirit would remain with them forever and would remind them of who they were and what it meant for them to be God's people. The Spirit would also remind them of who Jesus was and what he had taught. The Holy Spirit would also be the source of peace. Jesus offered words of comfort when he said, "I will not leave you orphaned" (John 14:18).

John's Gospel uses a term that can be translated as "advocate" to talk about this role of the Spirit. The term can be misleading for us because we may not hear the legal overtones. A lawyer can be an advocate, giving voice to truth in a persuasive way to convince those who hear. This is the kind of advocate the Holy Spirit was to be for the disciples and for us—a voice that would continue to speak truth when people's understanding of truth might be confused or lost.

One of the most important functions of the Spirit would be the continuation of Jesus' message. Everything that the disciples would need could not be spelled out before Jesus' death. They couldn't process it all or understand what it all meant until they had experienced the impact of Jesus' death and resurrection. The Holy Spirit would carry on Jesus' teaching ministry; and if they would trust what Jesus had said about love and how to live, then they would continue to experience new revelations through the work of the Holy Spirit.

How does Jesus' reassurance about the continuing and guiding presence of the Holy Spirit offer comfort to Christians today? What might his reassurance to his followers mean for you?

REFLECT

Bible Facts

The Greek word that appears as "advocate" in some translations of John 14:6 is paraclete, *which has a range of meanings including "counselor," "helper," "comforter," or "intercessor." Its most general meaning is "one who comes to the aid of someone else."*

Our Work With the Holy Spirit
Matthew 28:19-20; Luke 24:44-49

Jesus clearly saw that his ministry was not going to end with his death and resurrection. There was going to be work to do. You might ask, "What sort of work? After all, if God had done everything that God intended to do to save the world through Jesus, why should there be anything more for us to do? What more could we add to what Jesus did on the cross? Anything else would surely be superfluous! How would we be empowered to do the work?"

What's in the Bible?

Read Matthew 28:19-20 and Luke 24:44-49. What particularly stands out for you in these Scriptures? Why? What did Jesus ask the disciples to do? What did he promise?

Both of these passages record some of the final instructions that Jesus gave to his disciples before departing from them. The Luke passage refers to being clothed with power from on high, which is probably a reference to the coming of the Holy Spirit at Pentecost, recorded in Acts 2.

History did not end when Jesus ascended back into the heavens, though. Like Elijah's mantle fell to Elisha (2 Kings 2), so Jesus' commission fell to those who had been following him. Even though the central event had already happened—the unveiling of God's salvation in the cross and empty tomb of Jesus—the Holy Spirit was going to continue to inspire and empower the disciples to tell the story and to teach and to baptize new followers. The Holy Spirit was going to empower them to imitate Jesus in their lives and in their life together in the world. It was one more way in which God demonstrated extravagance. God was not content to do salvation for us and then move right along to the end of time. Like Mary welcoming the Holy Spirit and making space for God to come into the world, God created space for the church within time. The Holy Spirit invites us to live like Jesus, to share in his pouring out of his life for the sake of others, to live out of the good news of what God has done, and to celebrate it in myriad ways. What is the purpose of this time after the Resurrection? Living in and inviting others to live in new life offered through Jesus Christ.

Just off the English mainland in the North Sea is a place that has been a site of Christian pilgrimage for many centuries. Lindesfarne, or Holy Island, has always been remote and off the beaten track; but in the period of history often called the Dark Ages, it was a place where Celtic monks produced great works of art. The illuminated manuscripts now known as the Lindesfarne Gospels required painstaking work over many months and years to complete, but the detail of the calligraphy and the beauty of the script is as moving today as it was a millennium ago. What purpose did it serve for those monks to labor so intensively on these books? For them it was of a piece with the worship and hospitality that they also offered. All of it was given to God.

There are lots of seemingly pointless things that fill our lives. Surely there were many who questioned the disciples about the new lifestyle that they adopted after throwing in their lot with Jesus. What purpose did their prayer and worship and teaching serve? For them it was a way of following in the footsteps of Jesus, not always knowing why or where these practices would lead but trusting in the Holy Spirit to reveal the path. Are the things we fill our lives with pointless or are they pointing toward something greater than ourselves?

Make a list of the things you have done in the last 24 hours. Which activities seem trivial to you? Which seem meaningful to you? Which would seem trivial or meaningful to others? If you were living up to the instruction and promise Jesus gave to the disciples, which activities would you change? What would you add to the list?

REFLECT

Prayer and the Holy Spirit
Luke 10:21-22; 11:1-13

The readings in Luke deal with Jesus' teachings about prayer, one of the primary ways we enter into relationship with God through the Holy Spirit.

What's in the Bible?
Read Luke 10:21-22; 11:1-13. What stands out for you in these Scriptures? What does Jesus teach his followers about prayer? What do the Scriptures tell you about Jesus, the Holy Spirit, and prayer?

One way that the Holy Spirit has been understood is as a witness to the love of the Father for the Son, Jesus. If we were to imagine the Trinity in this way, we might see the Holy Spirit pulsing with energy, hovering, if you will, between the Father and the Son. The Spirit infuses the Trinity with a vibrancy that keeps up a vital communication of love. It is no wonder that when the Gospel of John tells us that Jesus rejoiced in prayer to God, it tells us that he rejoiced "in the Holy Spirit" (Luke 10:21). The Spirit was a true witness to what was going on in Jesus' heart. The free and easy way that Jesus talks in prayer is open to all who seek the Holy Spirit. The Spirit then sweeps us up into the life of the Trinity where we can also experience the vibrancy and love that is at the heart of the universe.

In Luke 11:1-4, we find the model prayer of Jesus that also occurs in Matthew 6:9-13. Here we see the expression of God's holiness, the prayer for God's kingdom to be realized on earth, the prayer for daily needs, the prayer for forgiveness and for the power to forgive, and the prayer for deliverance from the time of trial. The prayer presupposes a life of relationship with God that leads to the capacity to live as God intends. Next we find a section about persistence in prayer (Luke 11:5-8). The reading concludes with words of assurance about prayer, assurance that points directly to the Holy Spirit. "How much more will the heavenly Father give the Holy Spirit to those who ask him!" (verse 13). The aim of prayer, ultimately, is relationship with the Holy Spirit of God. Paul elaborates the life-giving presence of the Holy Spirit within the believer in Romans 8; and in this chapter, he speaks profoundly about prayer: "Likewise the Spirit helps us in our weakness; for we do not know how to pray as we ought, but that very Spirit intercedes with sighs too deep for words" (Romans 8:26).

How does the Lord's Prayer speak to you? What does this Scripture say to you about praying for specific needs? What does it say to you about the aim of prayer? about the presence of the Holy Spirit?

REFLECT

Guidance for a New Day
Acts 6:1-7; 13:1-5

When the Holy Spirit exploded on the scene at Pentecost, the followers of Jesus were propelled from Jerusalem into the world. As they went, they faced new challenges that caused confusion and conflict. The community welcomed in all kinds of people, not just Jews. The duties of the leaders grew so that there were questions about who should be doing what. In the midst of these growing pains, the new church looked to the Holy Spirit for guidance.

What's in the Bible?
Read Acts 6:1-7; 13:1-5. What strikes you about the way these early followers of Jesus made decisions? Why? What does the Scripture say to you about the presence of the Holy Spirit with God's people?

Acts 6:1-7 describes a dispute over who was going to ensure that food was distributed equitably to those in need. In order to resolve the dispute, the community appointed new leaders who shared a particular quality: They were full of the Holy Spirit and wisdom. Later, as described in Acts 13:1-5, we see a glimpse of the church in Antioch and how it listened to God through worship and fasting. The Holy Spirit directed them to choose new leaders for a new mission. These episodes show that the Christian community was developing specific practices to help them be open to what the Holy Spirit was saying. Jesus was no longer there in body, but he was still leading them through changing circumstances through the presence and guidance of the Holy Spirit.

How do groups that you are in respond to new challenges? If you were to follow the Acts examples for seeking the Holy Spirit's guidance, what would you have to do individually? as a group?

Recognizing the Spirit
Galatians 5:16-25

The Christian church didn't always live up to its highest ideals. Like every human organization, it was prone to dissension and moral failures. Much of Paul's communication with the churches he established was directed at problems that had developed within the communities. The letters of Paul are a record of those dynamic but troubled times. In Galatians we find his description of the Spirit-led life.

What's in the Bible?

Read Galatians 5:16-25. What images or phrases speak to you in these passages? Why? What does this Scripture say to you about a Spirit-led life? How do we know we are living as the Holy Spirit directs us?

Paul continually reminded the followers of Jesus that they were living in a new age, the age of the Spirit. Living in this age required a new way of life. Paul's shorthand for what needed to be left behind was "the flesh." He did not mean that the body in itself was evil. The flesh was created by God and was created good. The flesh was Paul's way of talking about the whole human person that needed to be redeemed. Such problems as sexual sins, jealousy, fighting, and the like were as much problems of the inner person as of the outer. The good news is that the Holy Spirit offers us a new way of life for our whole selves. We are not slaves to the worst that we can be, but we have a new freedom in Christ. In that freedom we find new capacities within ourselves. We find love, joy, peace, patience, kindness, generosity, faithfulness, gentleness, and self-control. When we discover these within ourselves, we are no longer in the flesh but in the Spirit, something that encompasses much more of who we are meant to be.

How are the fruit of the Spirit evident in the people you know? in you?

REFLECT

At Home in the Holy Spirit

The desire for home and connection is deep within each of us. When we feel disconnected from God and others, we feel the longing for a place where we are known and accepted. Too many people in this world are still searching for renewal, inspiration, and the power to live as children of God and not as throwaways. When we open our hearts and minds to God's presence and power through the Holy Spirit, we discover that we are home. We also discover the vitality and power we need to move into the future as the people of God.

Here's Why I Care

What place in you is waiting for renewal, inspiration, and power? Where is the Holy Spirit calling you to go?

A Prayer

Vibrant Holy Spirit, you wait at the doorway of my heart, ready to turn the world upside down. Let me be a space for your renewal to take hold. Send me into the future where you are already breathing new life. Amen.

APPENDIX
PRAYING THE BIBLE

Praying the Bible is an ancient process for engaging the Scriptures in order to hear the voice of God. It is also called *lectio divina*, which means "sacred reading." You may wish to use this process in order to become more deeply engaged with the Bible readings offered in each chapter of this study book. Find a quiet place where you will not be interrupted, a place where you can prayerfully read your Bible. Choose a Bible reading from a chapter in this study book. Use the following process to "pray" the Bible reading. After you pray the Bible reading, you may wish to record your experience in writing or through another creative response using art or music.

Be Silent

Open your Bible, and locate the Bible reading you have chosen. After you have found the reading, be still and silently offer all your thoughts, feelings, and hopes to God. Let go of concerns, worries, or agendas. Just *be* for a few minutes.

Read

Read the Bible passage slowly and carefully aloud or silently. Reread it. Be alert to any word, phrase, or image that invites you, intrigues you, confuses you, or makes you want to know more. Wait for this word, phrase, or image to come to you; and try not to rush it.

Reflect

Repeat the word, phrase, or image from the Bible reading to yourself and ruminate over it. Allow this word, phrase, or image to engage your thoughts, feelings, hopes, or memories.

Pray

Pray that God will speak to you through the word, phrase, or image from the Bible reading. Consider how this word, phrase, or image connects with your life and how God is made known to you in it. Listen for God's invitation to you in the Bible reading.

Rest and Listen

Rest silently in the presence of God. Empty your mind. Let your thoughts and feelings move beyond words, phrases, or images. Again, just *be* for a few minutes. Close your time of silent prayer with "Amen," or you may wish to end your silence with a spoken prayer.